D1061251

Garrett Book Company
MAR 2 6 2016

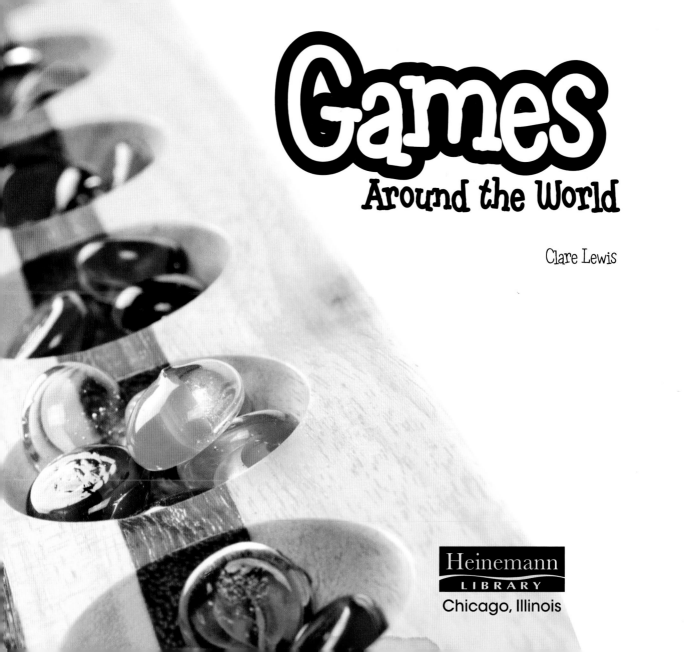

Games
Around the World

Clare Lewis

Heinemann
LIBRARY
Chicago, Illinois

© 2015 Heinemann Library
an imprint of Capstone Global Library, LLC
Chicago, Illinois

To contact Capstone Global Library, please
call 800-747-4992, or visit our web site
www.capstonepub.com

All rights reserved. No part of this publication may be
reproduced or transmitted in any form or by any means,
electronic or mechanical, including photocopying,
recording, taping, or any information storage and retrieval
system, without permission in writing from the publisher.

Edited by Joanna Issa, Shelly Lyons, Diyan Leake, and
Helen Cox Cannons
Designed by Cynthia Akiyoshi
Original illustrations © Capstone Global Library Ltd 2014
Picture research by Elizabeth Alexander and
Tracy Cummins
Production by Victoria Fitzgerald
Originated by Capstone Global Library Ltd
Printed and bound in China by Leo Paper Group

18 17 16 15 14
10 9 8 7 6 5 4 3 2 1

Library of Congress Cataloging-in-Publication Data
Lewis, Clare.
  Games around the world / Clare Lewis.
    pages cm.—(Around the world)
  Includes bibliographical references and index.
  ISBN 978-1-4846-0371-0 (hb)—ISBN 978-1-4846-0378-
9 (pb) 1. Games—Juvenile literature. 2. Games—Cross-
cultural studies—Juvenile literature. I. Title.

GV1203.L473 2015
790.1—dc23   2013040506

Acknowledgments
We would like to thank the following for permission
to reproduce photographs: Alamy pp. 4 (© Patrick
Eden), 6 (© View Stock), 8 & 22c (both © AHOWDEN
INTERNATIONAL), 12 & 22e (both © Peter Horree), 15 &
23 (both © Neil McAllister), 16 (© David Litschel); Getty
Images pp. 5 & 22a (both Manfred Gottschalk), 10 (David
Patrick Valera), 11 & 23 (both Jacek Chabraszewski),
13 & 22d (both Fuse), 17 (Simon Watson), 18 (Fabrice
LEROUGE), 20 (JGI/Jamie Grill), 21 (Tim Hall);
Shutterstock pp. 1 (© 2happy), 2 (© effe45), 3 (© pio3),
7 (© Kirk Peart Professional Imaging); Superstock pp.
9 (PhotoAlto), 14 (Chevalier Virginie / Oredia Eurl), 19
& 22b (both Travel Library Limited). Design elements
Shutterstock (© Tomislav Forgo, © Olga Popova, © Dan
Kosmayer, © Africa Studio, © RTimages, © STILLFX).

Cover photograph of Masai tribe member in Kenya
playing soccer reproduced with permission of SuperStock
(Ton Koene / age fotostock). Back cover photograph
reproduced with permission of Superstock (© Chevalier
Virginie / Oredia Eurl).

Every effort has been made to contact copyright holders
of material reproduced in this book. Any omissions will
be rectified in subsequent printings if notice is given to
the publisher.

All the Internet addresses (URLs) given in this book were
valid at the time of going to press. However, due to the
dynamic nature of the Internet, some addresses may
have changed, or sites may have changed or ceased to
exist since publication. While the author and publisher
regret any inconvenience this may cause readers, no
responsibility for any such changes can be accepted by
either the author or the publisher.

000000LEOF14

Contents

Games Everywhere

All around the world, children play games.

Grown-ups play games, too.

People play games for fun.

Sometimes people watch other people play games.

Games with Friends

People play games with
their friends.

Friends can play games with pens and paper.

Games Alone

People play games alone.

People play games on screens.

Different Types of Games

People play ball games.

People play soccer.

People play card games.

People play board games.

People play skipping games.

People play clapping games.

People play games with sticks.

People play games with stones.

People play make-believe games.

What games do you like to play?

Map of Games Around the World

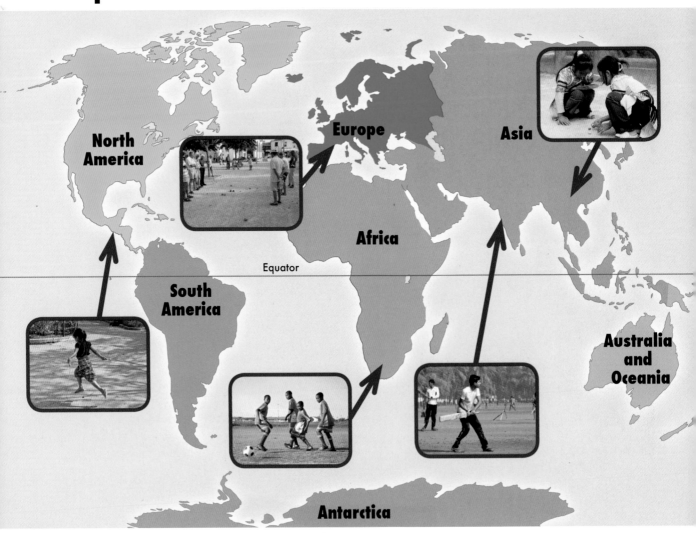

North America

Europe

Asia

Africa

South America

Equator

Australia and Oceania

Antarctica

Picture Glossary

board game game that has pieces that are moved along a board

screen part of a computer or tablet that you look at to see the pictures or writing

Index

Notes for parents and teachers

Before reading

Read the title of the book and then write the word *games* on the board. Ask children to name some games they know about, recording their answers as a list. Turn to page 24 of the book and explain that the index is a tool that helps readers find specific information in a book. Read the index entries and notice if there are any items that are similar to the list on the board. Demonstrate how to use the index to find the page where that type of game is mentioned.

After reading

- Review the list made before reading the book. Ask children if they learned about any other types of game from reading the book. Add them to the list.

- Turn to the map on page 22 and identify the seven continents with children. Discuss how this book is about games that are played all over the world, and demonstrate how this map is a tool that identifies where some of the photos were taken.

- Discuss that games often have rules that players must follow. Have children identify a familiar game (such as a game played at recess) and make a list of rules that they follow when they play the game. Depending on the age and ability of the children, you might have them work in pairs, or it could be a whole class activity.

McLennan County Public Library
Waco, Texas
Waco, TX 42040